CONTENTS

CHAPTER 1

THE FAITH DILEMMA

The nineteen-year-old preacher was crouched on a rock just behind the little country church. Desperate to remain unnoticed by the people entering through the front door he agonized, "Oh God, give me faith. I'm trying so hard to believe. How can I have the faith of those early disciples?" He was clenching his fists in turmoil until his knuckles began to turn white, sincerely pleading with God. That young preacher was me.

Oh, how I wanted to experience God's power just as I saw in the Book of Acts. The healing ministry of Jesus intrigued me. I wanted to see miracles, but I knew from Scripture I needed faith. Without faith it is impossible to please God, and I sure wanted my life to be pleasing to the Lord.

Many people feel they have some faith, <u>but not enough</u>. In spite of sincere attempts at producing faith, they find themselves coming up short time and again.

Others have experienced anguish over their perceived lack of faith; especially those sick and needy, who may feel that a miracle has eluded them due to their lack of faith. That's why I invite you to join me on a discovery. We will look at two people, the only two, to whom Jesus ascribed not only faith, but "great faith." By the time you finish the pages of this book you will be rejoicing because you will know that you too can enjoy this "great faith."

If you have received Jesus Christ as your Savior, you will see that you already have faith. God has dealt a measure of faith to every person (Roman 12:3). Just like a car must have an engine to be a car, a believer has faith; otherwise he is not a believer. The moment we respond to God's love through Jesus, He imparts faith to us. You will discover how the faith you already have will increase and flourish: it will be made easy. *Faith will flow through you as freely as the blood flowing through your veins*. This "great faith" will not depend on your performance, but instead it is fully wrapped up in Jesus. Once you experience this kind of faith, a new world of possibilities will open to you.

One of the two to whom Jesus ascribed great faith was a mother crying out for her child, and the other was a Roman military officer desperately looking for healing on behalf of a paralyzed servant. Who were these two? What were their secrets? What is "great faith?" How can we enjoy this kind of faith today?

Faith is the key to everything God has promised

us. Jesus stated that even the smallest measurement of faith, a grain of mustard seed, is enough to speak to a mountain of impossibilities and it will be moved. Consequently, to enjoy "great faith" is a key to God's unlimited blessings. We certainly want to know what "great faith" is, but more importantly, *how* do we get it?

The answers may surprise you. In fact, the two individuals Jesus referred to as having "great faith" didn't even seem to know that they had "great faith." Interestingly, they appear to be unaware that they had any faith at all, and neither one of them showed any concern about attaining faith. Still, Jesus said they had it.

THE STRUGGLE FOR FAITH

To some the issue of faith poses a dilemma. On the one hand, God is the Source of everything. Everything we need is already available by God. If we need healing, joy, prosperity, blessings or miracles, God has all of these for us and the Bible gives us numerous promises about God's willingness to give. Jesus said, "Ask, and you shall receive." James writes, "You have not because you ask not." Jesus states that God's willingness to give far exceeds that of a parent desiring to give good things to their children. "If you then, being evil, know how to give good gifts to your children, how much more will your heavenly Father *give* the Holy Spirit to those who ask Him!" (Luke 11:13)

If God is willing to give to us, then why are some not receiving? This is a valid question. You may have heard the statement, "God is not the problem: we are." Let's examine this statement for a moment. First, God has never changed. Jesus is the same yesterday, today and forever. When we read of Jesus' ministry, He never refused healing or blessing to anyone who came sincerely asking of Him. Jesus was never the problem.

Are we at times the problem? Yes, without a question. The only instance that someone did not receive a miracle from Jesus was because of their own unbelief, as was the case with the people in Jesus' hometown of Nazareth. Jesus marvelled at their unbelief and He could not do any mighty miracle there. Jesus was not the problem; the people of Nazareth were.

However, in what way could we be a problem, since all we want is to receive from God, and He is willing to give to us? We need to be careful that this statement, "God is not the problem: we are," does not lead to self-loathing and condemnation which are never from God. Jesus stated very clearly that He did not come to condemn people (John 3:17). We may erroneously surmise that we ought to look within ourselves to see what hindrances to faith may be in us. Introspection will not produce positive results or miracles in our lives. I caution you that to look inwardly will only lead to disappointment and insecurity. True miracles are only found in looking to Jesus Christ. The problem of the people of Nazareth was simply that they did not view Jesus properly. If they had only recognized Him for who He is, they could have received the same miracles people in other towns enjoyed.

Frequently people will question, "Why don't I have the blessings of God, especially since He wants to give them to me?" Many determine the problem is their own lack of faith, questioning how they can acquire more faith in order to access the promises they have heard are readily available from God. This idea of lacking faith is reinforced by people who tell you, "Well, you need more faith." At times the struggle for this elusive quality called faith seems endless.

People study the principles of faith: reading and confessing God's Word, visualizing God's promises, rebuking the devil, and so on. When the answers to their prayers still elude them, they are told repeatedly, "You need more faith," and so their struggle heightens.

Some work very hard at controlling what they say so as not to speak anything negative. Others put Scripture verses on prominent display in their home and car to always remind them of what God has said. This is important and good. I also display Scripture verses and statements by Jesus to keep them ever before me. However sadly, some do everything they can possibly think of to do, and yet still it seems nothing is happening. Faith appears increasingly to be an enigma or a mystery. "How can I get faith to work in my life?" becomes the nagging question.

If you pay attention to the words of Jesus, you notice how important faith is. Jesus rebuked the disciples for their lack of faith. His words were, "Oh ye of little faith," or "Why do you have no faith?" In fact, the only time you see Jesus slightly irritated is when He notices lack of faith in the disciples. So much more reason for us to pursue faith, since we certainly do not want to frustrate Jesus.

The Book of Hebrews says, "But without faith it is impossible to please Him, for he who comes to God must believe that He is, and that He is a rewarder of those who diligently seek Him." (Hebrews 11:6) Again, we are faced with the crucial necessity of faith.

THE "FAITH POLICE"

Some may have encountered what I call the "faith police." These are individuals who think they have great faith and like to point out lack of faith in others. They seem to have all the answers and explanations for those who have seemingly not received an answer to their prayers. "You were not healed because you need more faith," is their explanation. These individuals are often well-intentioned, but their words still condemn others for not thinking, confessing or imagining the promises of God as they should. The problem is further compounded because many of these "faith police" do not themselves enjoy the blessings of God. When they face impossible circumstances they also become discouraged and find themselves unable to obtain the answer to their prayers.

Do you see the perpetual problem we encounter on this treadmill of the pursuit of faith? The more we try to have faith, the more it seems we never quite have it. It seems as elusive as the rainbow. You see the rainbow in the distance with its beautiful colors and majestic arch; yet as you race toward it, it vanishes out of sight completely unattainable. Some simply give up. You can hear them sigh, "Faith is not for me. It works for others, but I can't get it to work in my life."

MOVING MOUNTAINS

Jesus said, "Assuredly, I say to you, if you have faith as a mustard seed, you will say to this mountain, 'Move from here to there,' and it will move; and nothing will be impossible for you." (Matthew 17:20)

There is no ambiguity in Jesus' words. Faith in the mere size of a mustard seed will enable you to speak to a mountain to move, and it will move. We must take Jesus' words at face value. There are only two possible explanations of His statement. Either Jesus was telling the truth or He wasn't. Since Jesus is the truth, what are we to make of the fact that many people claim to have faith, but their "mountain" has not moved? Could it be that what we may have called "faith" is not the kind of faith Jesus spoke of at all?

At times people confuse the God-kind of faith, mountain-moving faith, with mental believing.

The difference between faith and mental believing is like night and day. Mental believing is exercised by every person on a daily basis. Our whole system of society whether banking, postal service, or business is built on mental believing. When we open a box of cereal to eat breakfast, we do not logically and scientifically scrutinize every fiber or every flake; we believe what the package claims about the content. When we drop an envelope in the mailbox, we believe it will be delivered. With little exception, when we hear something on the radio, television, or read it in a newspaper we believe it to be true. This kind of believing has to do with the mind. It is metaphysical, which means it has to do with reason, logic and mental comprehension. Obviously it is not the kind of "faith" Jesus is speaking about when He refers to faith as a grain of mustard seed, the kind which enables you to speak to a mountain and it will move.

Jesus doesn't say that if you have faith as a grain of mustard seed, you will *at times* be able to move mountains. No, Jesus makes a blanket statement that "Nothing will be impossible for you," and the mountain "will move." This seems totally unrealistic and illogical to natural thinking. After repeated attempts at exercising this kind of faith some shrug it off saying, "It doesn't work for me."

In many churches today if the pastor were to announce a series of teachings on faith, there would be little excitement. The reason being, that people have already heard numerous teachings on faith and feel disillusioned when it has not worked as told to them it should.

I have seen thousands of people healed: the lame, blind, deaf, mute, lepers, cancer cases, humanly impossible cases. At the same time I walked away from many a service with shouts of rejoicing echoing in my ears as people celebrated the miracles that happened. I rejoiced with the others, but in my mind's eye I could also vividly see those who had not been healed. My heart ached for them. I have seen the lame walk, but I have also witnessed scenes where concerned Christians gathered around a wheelchair encouraging the sick person, rebuking the devil, even lifting the suffering one out of the wheelchair and trying to get them to walk only to have to put them back in the chair.

This is a far cry from Jesus, who said that faith in the smallest measurement conceivable meant "nothing will be impossible."

I don't claim to know everything, but the truths I share in this book are answers to questions I have had. My own soul has been satisfied by the answers I bring to you. Jesus has ministered these truths to me and faith has become easy. When we cease our pursuit of faith and allow the sweet presence of Jesus to flow through us, astounding miracles happen. All things are possible when Jesus' own faith becomes our faith. *This is the only faith that works.*

JESUS' OWN FAITH

The apostle Paul said, "I live by the faith *of* the Son of God." There is a giant step between faith in Christ and the faith *of* Christ. It was no longer the apostle's attempt at having faith in Christ, but now the very faith of Christ had become his. Simon Peter gives a similar testimony when he explains how the lame man was healed not by Simon Peter's faith or holiness, but by the faith that works through Jesus (Acts 3:16).

Maybe you, my reader, have struggled and wondered what could be the obstacle in your life. Possibly you have been encouraged to look inwardly to discover and root out hindrances. A lady recently approached me, "Pastor Peter, I am concerned that there are hindrances in me and that's why my family is not enjoying healing." I responded gently to her, "Surely there are hindrances in you, and furthermore there are hindrances in me and in every person that ever sought for God's healing and miracle supply. In fact, we could find some hindrance in every person if we looked hard enough. However, we are not to research and try to discern the hindrances within us because we will only discover more and more reasons why we should not experience the blessings of God." I continued, "Rather, we look at Jesus in whom there are no hindrances. All the promises of God are ours in Christ Jesus, not on the basis of what we have done, but because of Him." God's promises are received by us, not because of our obedience, but because of Jesus' obedience.

This is what Paul proclaimed, "For the Son of God, Jesus Christ, who was preached among you…was not Yes and No, but in Him was Yes. For all the promises of God in Him are Yes, and in Him Amen, to the glory of God through us." (2 Corinthians 1:19-20) Notice that

God's promises are "yes" and "amen" in Jesus. This way God gets all the glory as He works through us. We cannot credit our own diligence or any goodness in us, but all the credit goes to the Lord Jesus Christ.

IT'S DIFFERENT IN THE NEW TESTAMENT

Don't construe my words to mean that we should not obey God's Word. On the contrary, when we discover the promises of God are already ours in Jesus, we will want to be even more obedient to His Word. In the Old Testament, before the death and resurrection of Jesus, people tried to obey God in order to obtain His promises. We, who live in the New Testament after the death and resurrection of Jesus, do not work to obtain God's promises. These promises are already ours because of what Jesus has done. We obey God, not to obtain His favor, but because all God's favor belongs to us in Jesus.

In the Old Testament people made sacrifices and prayers in order to obtain blessings from God, while now in the New Testament we do things because of all Christ has done for us. They were obedient to God in order to please Him; we are obedient to God because He has saved us and given us a new life. God is now pleased because of what Jesus has done.

Before Jesus' death and resurrection, people petitioned God for His blessings. This kind of prayer is no longer appropriate because the apostle Paul says, "Blessed be the God and Father of our Lord Jesus Christ, who has blessed us with every spiritual blessing in the heavenly places in Christ." (Ephesians 1:3) Here we clearly see that God already has blessed us with every spiritual blessing. We don't need to ask for that which we already have. This is an eye-opener to many. God has already blessed us. Now the proper prayer is to thank God for the blessings we have in Christ. When everything around us looks dark and hopeless, we still praise God for what His Word says we already have.

At times we need to ask the Holy Spirit to open our eyes to see what we have *now*. Paul the apostle prayed, "The eyes of your understanding being enlightened; that you may know what is the hope of His calling, what are the riches of the glory of His inheritance in the saints, and what is the exceeding greatness of His power toward us who believe, according to the working of His mighty power." (Ephesians 1:18-19) Do you see the stark difference? In the Old Testament people prayed in order to get blessed. Now in the New Covenant, we ask God to show us more clearly the inheritance we already have.

In order to have great faith it is very important to recognize which side of the cross we live in. We live after the cross; Jesus has already put away the world's sins and carried our sicknesses. This is vastly different from life prior to Christ's death and resurrection. Christ's righteousness has now been credited to our account, and on the basis of His righteousness we inherit all of God's goodness and promises.

We no longer love in order to obtain God's love; we love God because He first loved us. We pray *not* to obtain the victory or the blessing, but because the victory is already ours in Christ. Similarly, we don't try to have faith by our own effort, but *we have faith because we are linked with the author and the finisher of our faith, who is Jesus Christ Himself.*

The two individuals who enjoyed "great faith" connected with Jesus and saw their "mountains" move. How did they tap into this Jesus-kind of faith? What was their secret? The purpose of this book is to help the reader discover Jesus just like the two people who had "great faith" discovered Him. Almost invariably before I preach or even speak one-on-one with a needy person, I ask the Holy Spirit to reveal Jesus to people. My best sermons will be ineffective and my prayers will be powerless unless Jesus is clearly shown to people. That's my prayer for you, that the Holy Spirit will reveal Jesus, and that He will become big to you.

CHAPTER 2

TWO WITH "GREAT FAITH"

Many individuals in the Gospels are described as having faith, but only two with "great faith."

Jesus had entered His hometown of Capernaum when a Roman military official approached Him, "Lord, my servant is lying at home, paralyzed and dreadfully tormented." Jesus immediately responded, "I will come and heal him." The Roman centurion couldn't ask for more than that. Jesus was completely willing and available to visit his home. The centurion responded, "Lord, I am not worthy that You should come under my roof. But only speak a word, and my servant will be healed. For I also am a man under authority, having soldiers under me. And I say to this one, 'Go,' and he goes; and to another, 'Come,' and he comes; and to my servant, 'Do this,' and he does it." Jesus marveled at the centurion's words, "Assuredly, I say to you, I have not found such <u>great faith</u>, not even in Israel!" (Matthew 8:8-10)

The account concludes with Jesus saying, " 'Go your way; and as you have believed, so let it be done for you.'

And his servant was healed that same hour." (Matthew 8:13)

Jesus "marveled," which means to "gaze in wonder." It denotes total astonishment. Jesus was unaccustomed to this kind of faith, and He had never seen it in Israel.

The second person with great faith is found a few chapters later in the Gospel of Matthew:

> "Then Jesus went out from there and departed to the region of Tyre and Sidon. And behold, a woman of Canaan came from that region and cried out to Him, saying, 'Have mercy on me, O Lord, Son of David! My daughter is severely demon-possessed.' But He answered her not a word. And His disciples came and urged Him, saying, 'Send her away, for she cries out after us.' But He answered and said, 'I was not sent except to the lost sheep of the house of Israel.' Then she came and worshiped Him, saying, 'Lord, help me!' But He answered and said, 'It is not good to take the children's bread and throw it to the little dogs.' And she said, 'Yes, Lord, yet even the little dogs eat the crumbs which fall from their masters' table.' Then Jesus answered and said to her, 'O woman, great is your faith! Let it be to you as you desire.' And her daughter was healed from that very hour." (Matthew 15:21-28)

Again Jesus states, "great is your faith." What was it about this desperate woman that constituted extraordinary faith? Are there differences between her and the Roman centurion? What are the common denominators? How can we learn from them?

Before we answer these questions, let's look at what "great faith" is not. If we look for faith in the wrong direction we'll come up empty. I don't claim to know everything. I know that I am nothing in myself, but the Lord Jesus Christ has poured this understanding of faith into my heart by His grace. I've spent more than thirty years in Gospel ministry, and all throughout those years God has blessed me. Still today, I vividly recall the first tangible healing of a deaf person that I witnessed as a nineteen-year-old preacher conducting a three-week conference in Toronto, Canada. It shocked me. I knew this was something real.

SOMETHING MISSING

Still, in spite of witnessing thousands of healings, I've also been keenly aware of those whose prayers seem to go unanswered and I have wondered, "Why?" There didn't seem to be any difference in the sincerity between those who received their healing and those who seemed to walk away with their prayers unanswered. I heard many explanations and tried to come up with some myself. Well-meaning people asked me, "Peter, why do a lot more miracles happen overseas?" I never agreed with the question because I have visited many churches overseas, seeing no more happen there than I've witnessed in North America or Europe. God is not greater in one location than another. Furthermore I have seen great miracles in Europe and North America.

"The faith level is just too low," is another logical explanation that I have heard and sometimes used myself. I've heard preachers recommend to a sick person, "You must read more healing books and listen to more teaching tapes on faith." I have given the same advice. Still inwardly, I knew I was missing something.

You will discover that the key to faith is to cease from all our pursuits after faith, and instead connect with Him who is our faith, Jesus Christ, the author and finisher of faith (Hebrews 12:2). As you allow the Holy Spirit to minister this to your heart, the faith of Jesus will increasingly flow through you. In Him you will find the answers that you may have sought for a long time.

WHAT GREAT FAITH IS NOT

Much has been made of the fact that the Roman centurion was "under authority" because he said, "For I also am a man under authority." The topic of spiritual authority is crucial and I don't want to minimize that. When we teach spiritual leadership, we focus on the truth that to have authority one must be under authority. To be a leader, one has to learn how to be a good follower. However, our study here is not leadership, but faith for miracles. The centurion was not making a statement about spiritual leadership. He only described how he saw his own authority as an illustration of Jesus' authority. Just like a military commander speaks and the soldiers obey so Jesus speaks and sickness, demons and circumstances must obey!

To claim that somehow the centurion attained to his miracle by understanding the need for submission to authority is false, and not in line with what this account tells us. I can prove this by looking at the Canaanite woman. She appears void of understanding submission to authority. Actually, she seems rebellious. When Jesus at first ignores her request for a miracle, she refuses to submit to Jesus' silence. When the disciples urged Jesus, "Send her away for she cries after us," again she doesn't get the hint (Matthew 15:23). The story indicates that she was a nuisance to the disciples. They wanted her to leave, but she refused to come under the disciples' "authority."

I'm not suggesting we should rebel against authority: not at all. I'm merely pointing out that whether a person has been under human authority or not does not qualify or disqualify someone to receive a miracle. Let me be quick to say again that I believe in authority. In our ministry we practice submitting to authority. When I visit a local church, I submit to the leader in charge of that congregation. Submitting to authority, whether spiritual or governmental, is scriptural.

Let me remove a weight from you, my sick or needy friend. Maybe you have struggled to receive a miracle from God, and when it seemed elusive you condemned yourself, blaming the lack of result on some inadequacy on your part. Possibly, you blamed the lack of answered prayer on some flaw in your past. Maybe you lived a rebellious lifestyle and now you view this as an obstacle to God's blessings. Your miracle will never come by looking to your failures or past shortcomings. When looking at yourself you will only distance yourself from God's provision.

PUSHING FOR YOUR BREAKTHROUGH!?

Some have suggested that the Canaanite woman's "great faith" was her insistence, pushing for her miracle against all odds. This idea of "pushing for your breakthrough," or "pressing in," or "pressing through," has been presented to many a needy person. In the case of seriously sick or dying individuals, this emphasis can be dangerous. Imagine a dying person carried into a healing service. The person has tried every means of recovery – doctors, medicines, natural remedies, but in spite of all effort the doctor has pronounced the death sentence: "You only have a month to live." This desperate person now hears that in order to receive a miracle from God you must push for your breakthrough. The sick person is told they must take a stand against unbelief and break fear in their life. While these statements contain truths, this focus becomes a heavy burden for an already desperate person.

I propose to you that the key to the miracle of this Canaanite woman was <u>not</u> her "pushing for a breakthrough." The evidence of this is found in the account of the Roman centurion. He did not push for a miracle at all. On the contrary, he was relaxed, even laid back. Jesus offered to come to his house and heal the servant, but the centurion was not anxious for any special visit by Jesus. Should not the centurion have "pushed" with all his might for Jesus to come to his house as a sure way to a miracle? Instead, the centurion was relaxed, not looking for any special visit or touch from Jesus. He knew Jesus is so great that it would be enough if He would "speak the word only."

Being pushy for your miracle is not wrong or right in and of itself. I'm merely showing it is not a common denominator for "great faith." The Canaanite woman was pushy; the Roman centurion was not. If someone is pushy or demanding for prayer, it may indicate a sense of panic; faith and panic never work together.

Maybe you have blamed your lack of receiving from not pushing hard enough for your miracle. You condemn yourself for not trying hard enough. This may have become a burden around your neck as you push yourself ever harder to attain your miracle. Perhaps you are struggling, shouting rebukes at the devil and faith commands at yourself, and still nothing is happening. Be at rest, there is a better way. You can have great faith, but it doesn't come by our effort, struggles or our spiritual performance. Let the weight of human inadequacy fall from you. No miracle of God has ever come because of what we strive to do, but only because of what Jesus has done.

To insist or push in your own strength for God to give you something has nothing to do with receiving your miracle. Every outstanding miracle I have witnessed has come with great peace. There's never been the case of us rolling up our "spiritual" sleeves and getting into heavy-duty boisterous screaming and rebuking of the devil. When we try to make a miracle happen, we come up empty; just like Jesus' disciples who fished all night and caught nothing. Our own efforts don't produce results. Instead, we are left disappointed, with perplexing questions and at times physically exhausted.

In every one of our Gospel Festivals we see scores of lame, deaf and blind healed, not once in a while, but consistently. If I were to draw a single truth about faith out of these experiences, it would be that the greater the peace and the rest, the less we struggle and the more actually happens. The more we try to make it happen, the less we see tangible results.

Interestingly, we find some contradictions between the behavior of the Roman centurion and the Canaanite woman. One was pushy; the other one was laid back. One seemed to understand submission to authority; the other one did not. Yet neither of these characteristics seemed to have any bearing on their ability to have great faith. Now let's look at what these two with "great faith" have in common.

CHAPTER 3

GREAT FAITH IS A GREAT JESUS

The middle-aged man beside me was excited. He had been blind for several years and now Jesus had opened his eyes. The crowd in the soccer stadium in northern Papua New Guinea listened intently before they responded with shouts of joy. When I asked the man, "Did you get healed during the prayer here tonight?" it became even more intriguing. He responded, "No, I was healed last night in my kitchen at home. You see, Mr. Youngren, I live in a village and many of the people from my area were here at your Gospel Festival. When they returned home they were excitedly reporting what God had done. I was so overwhelmed at their report that after they left my house I simply called out, 'Jesus, come and heal me now.' Right there all by myself I was healed, and I thought I should come and report to you what Jesus did."

That man had faith, but what exactly was that faith? He took the limits off Jesus as he looked beyond the preacher and discovered the greatness of Jesus. His healing was not limited to our meeting in the stadium where I was preaching. Instead, it was all about Jesus.

The greater Jesus is to you, the greater your faith. All evidence indicates that the people who received miracles in the Gospels did not know they had faith. The two to whom "great faith" was ascribed were equally ignorant. Nowhere do we see an example of someone approaching Jesus saying, "Lord, I have faith in You so now go ahead and heal me." This is just like the man in Papua New Guinea. He was not concerned about having great faith; his only focus was how great Jesus is.

Have we put such focus on acquiring faith that people are seeking it, rather than pursuing the Source of faith? *Faith doesn't come by seeking after faith; it comes from Jesus.*

Paul writes, "So then faith comes by hearing, and hearing by the word of God." (Romans 10:17) When you look in the context you see that the "hearing" referred to is when we hear of Jesus Christ and His death and resurrection. We are saved when we believe in our heart that God raised Jesus from the dead (v. 9). Do you see how faith is connected to Jesus? It is not isolated to believing in a word, idea or doctrine. Faith is directly connected to the person of Jesus. The word we hear, which builds our faith, is the word about Jesus Christ and what He has done.

Faith is not in your mind; it is in your heart. We cannot manufacture this kind of faith no matter how hard we try. When we willingly come to Jesus Christ, He imparts His faith to us. It is two sides of the same coin. On the one hand, Jesus is our faith. On the other hand, when we come to Him, He imparts His faith to us. We are saved by grace through faith. Faith is not of ourselves or from our effort; it is a gift of God (Ephesians 2:8-9). This idea is revolutionary. If this truth sinks into our hearts, faith will never again be the same to us.

FAITH IS "BETTER" NOW

In Hebrews chapter eleven we see a long list of faith heroes. Sometimes this chapter has been called, "Faith's Hall of Fame." Abel, Enoch, Noah, Abraham, Sarah, Isaac, Jacob, Joseph, Moses and others are given as examples of faith. What constituted faith for these "faith heroes?" Faith to them was obedience to a divine word. Amazingly, we are never told anywhere to imitate these "faith heroes." Some have looked at Hebrews chapter eleven and struggled to live up to the achievements of these great men and women of the past. On the contrary, the chapter ends, "And all these, having obtained a good testimony through faith, did not receive the promise, God having provided *something better* for us, that they should not be made perfect apart from us." (Hebrews 11:39-40)

What is this "*something better*?" The answer comes one verse later, "Looking unto Jesus, the author and finisher of (our) faith…" (Hebrews 12:2) The Old Testament people are commendable for how they obeyed a divine word; however, this is not the way we exercise faith. We have a better way. We connect directly with Jesus, the author and finisher of faith. We have a relationship with Him. He is the indwelling Christ in us (Colossians 1:27).

This truth is in line with the theme of the whole Book of Hebrews. The key word is "better." Jesus is better than the angels, and better than Aaron and Moses. The voice of God's Son is better than the voice of the prophets, and His blood is better than that of goats and calves. We have a better High Priest than the one in the Old Testament and the New Covenant is better than the one which came through Moses. This doesn't mean that the angels, Aaron, or the blood of goats and calves were bad. The writer of Hebrews doesn't suggest that the prophets were evil or bad; not in the least. All of these had their place, but Jesus is better.

There is no indication that the writer of Hebrews is suddenly changing the theme when he comes to chapter eleven. The list of Old Testament heroes are given in contrast to that which is better. We don't exercise faith the way they did because we have something better – we have the faith of Jesus. This is not a critique of the Old Testament heroes. On the contrary, they believed God according to what was available in their time, but our time is different. We live after the death and resurrection of Christ. Faith is "better" now. We have much more than a divine word; *we have Jesus Himself.*

FAITH OF CHRIST

Faith *in* Christ is good, but the faith *of* Christ is greater. Look again at the apostle Paul's words, "I live by the faith of the Son of God." (Galatians 2:20 KJV)

Some translations have written, "faith in Christ" but the King James Version of the Bible accurately says, "faith of Christ." Faith of Christ is the only rendition of the verse that makes sense. Paul says we are crucified with Christ, and a "crucified" person is dead. The only hope for such a person is that the life of another is lived through him. We have been crucified with Jesus Christ, and now He lives in us with His wisdom, faith and love.

This is the awesome key to the entire life of a believer in Jesus. We have become new creations in Christ (2 Corinthians 5:7). We are recreated in the image of God. Our life can never please God, but we have died from the old life. Instead, we have the glorious opportunity to yield to Jesus and allow His righteousness, love, joy and faith to flow through us. The apostle Simon Peter called it, "the faith which comes through Him." (Acts 3:16)

Faith was not the product of Simon Peter's effort. No, the miracle-working faith Simon Peter experienced was all wrapped up in Jesus; faith which "comes through Him." *The greater Jesus is to you, the greater your faith*. If your faith seems small, focus on Jesus more. Ask Him to help, strengthen and heal you.

DISCOVER THE HEALER

The Roman centurion and the Canaanite woman had a great Jesus. The centurion thought Jesus was so great that "a word" from Him would be enough for the miracle to occur. Though Jesus had already offered to come to the centurion's home, the centurion recommended otherwise. Why? He obviously thought Jesus is so great that a potentially arduous journey was unnecessary. Instead, "a word" was sufficient.

This event is a picture of the unlimited Jesus. It is as if the centurion was saying, "Jesus, You're so great; You don't have to come to my house. Just like I speak to a subordinate to go and he goes, come and he comes, when You release Your word, the sickness in my servant must leave."

The centurion had come for *healing*, but instead he saw *the Healer*. Jesus was so much greater than he could have ever imagined. All around there were those who wanted to limit Jesus saying things like, "We know Jesus. He's from Nazareth. He's Joseph's son, nothing special." In that sea of unbelief and negative comments, the centurion's voice rises above all others. He sees Jesus for who He really is. Jesus is so great, that no matter what the obstacle in your way, at His touch it will melt like the snow melts in the warm rays of the sun.

Look at the Canaanite woman. At first, Jesus doesn't respond to her request for the healing of her daughter. He states, "I was not sent except to the lost sheep of the house of Israel" (Matthew 15:24). When the woman keeps insisting Jesus responds, "It is not good to take the children's bread and throw it to the little dogs" (Matthew 15:26).

Here we see several interesting facts. First, *Jesus is still operating within the context of the Old Testament – "the house of Israel." The gospel had not yet gone global. That came after Jesus' death, resurrection, exaltation to heaven and the outpouring of the promised Holy Spirit. Today the power and life of Jesus is available to all who believe without limitations.*

Secondly, there is a clear delineation between the Old and the New Covenant. The woman is not Jewish and consequently not a part of God's covenant with the Jewish people. This distinction is never made after Jesus' death and the cross. Now all, whether Jew or Gentile, have access to God by the same covenant; the better covenant of Jesus Christ.

Finally, healing is the "bread of the children." Bread is a basic food. Healings and miracles are basic to those who embrace God's covenant in Jesus.

This woman could have been insulted by Jesus' seeming disinterest. In fact, Jesus' love was flowing toward her, but at the same time Jesus was respecting the fact that He was still in the Old Covenant. Jesus also knew that anyone, Jew or Gentile, could be healed by faith in Him. You who read this don't need to be concerned about the Old and the New Covenant. You are in the New Covenant, and the blessings of that covenant are yours. The important point for us to consider is how great Jesus was to the Canaanite woman. *She saw a great Jesus and Jesus saw "great faith."*

A CRUMB IS ENOUGH

It is worthwhile to point out that the Canaanite woman refused to be offended. Her response demonstrates how great Jesus was to her. She exclaims, "Yes, Lord, yet even the little dogs eat the crumbs which fall from their masters' table" (Matthew 15:27). Jesus' answer about healing being "bread of the children" may not have been the response she hoped for, but it was what she got; and she took it. It is as if she thought, "Well, I didn't get the answer I wanted, but Jesus said something, and I know His word is so reliable He will never back off from what He said!" Using Jesus' own expression, she makes it clear she doesn't need the whole loaf or even a slice of this "bread." Instead, a "crumb" is plenty. Why? She knew Jesus was so great that a "crumb" of His power was sufficient.

Great faith is not found in looking for great faith. Great faith is a great Jesus. See Him as great as He is. See His redemptive work and His love and power for you.

Stop trying to have faith, because faith doesn't come by trying. If you try to have faith and feel success in obtaining it, I regrettably inform you that what you got is not real faith. You may have a feeling of faith. You may talk, shout and jump like you would if you had real faith, but it's not the faith that produces miracles. That kind of faith comes not from trying to get it – it comes from Jesus Himself. You'll find real faith only in His presence.

This is so simple that many miss it altogether. Call on Jesus. Ask for His help. He will not fail you. Don't rely on theological beliefs or your years of Christian service. Approach Jesus like a child would his parent, expecting that He will give you mercy.

CHAPTER 4

FAITH OR MENTAL BELIEVING

There is a huge gap between mental believing and the God-kind of faith. Mental believing is natural. It comes by repeatedly telling our mind it is so. True faith is supernatural. It moves mountains and is only found in Jesus.

The four Gospels give us many case studies that contrast mental believing with the God-kind of faith. Matthew chapter seventeen begins with Jesus and three of His disciples on the Mount of Transfiguration. When they come down from the mountain, Jesus quickly encounters human pain and suffering. We read, "And when they had come to the multitude, a man came to Him, kneeling down to Him and saying, 'Lord, have mercy on my son, for he is an epileptic and suffers severely; for he often falls into the fire and often into the water. So I brought him to Your disciples, but they could not cure him.'" (Matthew 17:14-16)

Can you see the desperation? It's obvious Jesus' disciples believed in healing, otherwise they would not have tried to cure the boy. The father must have also believed in the miracle-working power of Jesus, because later he says, "Lord, I believe; help my unbelief!" (Mark 9:24)

We don't know all the details, but we can well imagine the disciples gathered around the boy while he was rolling on the ground, foaming at the mouth. Maybe they rebuked the devil or commanded the demons to leave and nothing happened. Possibly they tried repeatedly praying, interceding and pleading with God. Maybe they encouraged the father to believe more fervently, putting the onus for more faith on him or on the boy. Did the disciples try to discern the cause of the boy's sickness? Maybe they tried to research what had been the entry point for the demons to begin to oppress the boy and his family. We don't know exactly how they attempted to cure the boy, but we know they tried. Still, after all the prayer, rebuking and crying out to God was done, the result was dismal. The boy was as sick as ever before. Now some may conclude that this indicated it was not God's will to heal the boy. We know that's not the case because when Jesus came, He said, "Bring him here to Me." (Matthew 17:17) After a short conversation with the father, Jesus heals the boy. Jesus' action proves that it was God's will to heal the boy.

Later on, the disciples wonder at what they have seen and why they could not cure the boy. Jesus explains,

"Because of your unbelief; for assuredly, I say to you, if you have faith as a mustard seed, you will say to this mountain, 'Move from here to there,' and it will move; and nothing will be impossible for you." (Matthew 17:20)

A TRUCKLOAD OR A TEASPOON

Do you see the distinction between mental believing and mountain-moving faith? The disciples had exercised mental believing. No question! They believed in healing or they would not have attempted to cure the boy. Jesus shows that if they had real faith instead of mental believing they would only need a mustard seed of that kind of faith, and the miracle would happen.

A billion dollars worth of mental believing and nothing will happen, but a penny of faith, the God-kind of faith, and nothing is impossible.

What we call "faith" is often only mental believing or "mind over matter." People may be heard repeatedly saying, "I'm healed, I'm healed, I'm healed," or "I got it, I got it, I got it," or "It's mine, it's mine, it's mine." It is as if we thought that by repeating something enough we'll convince our own minds that we believe it, and then we'll get it.

The faith that Jesus gives, the God-kind of faith, is alive, vibrant and powerful. Let's never reduce faith to "five steps, ten keys, seven clues, or ten secrets." Faith can never be reduced to a mere principle or a "step." It is much more than affirming a doctrine; it is the energy of Jesus Himself flowing through you. Faith is not a condition of our mind; it is a divine grace.

A truckload of mental believing produced by human effort and struggle will do nothing, but a teaspoonful of the faith of Jesus will move mountains every time. The good news is that Jesus makes this faith readily available. You only have to come to Him, call out for Him, and draw near to Him. "But as many as received Him, to them He gave the right to become children of God, to those who believe in His name." (John 1:12) It's all wrapped up in "Him," "He" and "His." He does the work and we receive the benefits.

JUST AS I AM

In every Billy Graham crusade when the invitation for people to come to Christ is given the choir sings, "Just as I am without one plea, but that Thy blood was shed for me." I love those words, "without one plea." That means that I have nothing to plead of my own. I cannot brag of a single good thing about myself, including boasting of my faith. Instead, I simply come asking for God's mercy.

Remember the prayer meeting in the temple in Jerusalem with the publican in the back crying out for mercy, and the self-righteous Pharisee in the front of the sanctuary thanking God that he was not as "other sinners." Whose shoes would you rather be in: the publican sinner or the self-righteous Pharisee? There was no blessing in coming to God presenting something of ourselves, but mercy and grace flowed freely to the one who came "without one plea." All our mental attempts at faith will avail nothing. When we come to Jesus without anything of our own, the floodgates of His mercy and love open wide to us.

PEACE IN THE STORM

On another occasion when Jesus and the disciples were in the boat, a raging storm threatened to drown them. The disciples were on the deck crying out to God, commanding the winds to be calm, but nothing happened. Obviously they believed that God could calm the storm, but it was a believing produced of their mind. Jesus simply spoke the words, "Peace be still," and there was a great calm (Mark 4:39). This is the distinguishing mark between mental believing and the faith which comes of Jesus. Mental believing is our effort to believe and see something happen. Jesus' faith comes with great peace.

BELIEVE & SPEAK

Someone may ask, "Isn't it important that we speak in faith?" Yes, faith speaks and confesses God's Word. Our positive confession of God's Word comes from faith, but faith doesn't come from positive confession, for faith comes from Jesus. That's why the Scripture says, "I believe, therefore I spoke," not I spoke until I believed. You may ask, "Doesn't faith act?" Yes, action comes from faith, not faith from action – for faith only comes from Jesus.

VASCO'S NEW SHOES

While preaching in the central square in Plovdiv, Bulgaria a mother brought her five-year-old son, Vasco, who had been born paralyzed. The mother had heard of the wonders of Jesus that had happened in our previous meeting in Sofia, the capital of Bulgaria. She was overwhelmed with what she had heard, and now certain that her son would walk she bought him a pair of jeans, a jean jacket and a brand-new pair of sneakers. The boy had never owned a pair of shoes; he had no need for them as he could neither stand nor walk. However, Vasco's mother was sure he would need shoes because Jesus would heal him. As I preached Jesus that night a beaming five-year-old and a crying mother came on the platform. Vasco ran back and forth showing the people the wonder that had happened. The people were beside themselves with joy. That's the faith of Jesus in operation. He gave Vasco's mother mountain-moving faith.

Now I could tell that story and someone else who was lame could also buy new shoes and come to a meeting and nothing would happen. To the one person this was a living vibrant reality. To another person it may only be another faith technique. *Faith is not a method; faith is a person.*

THE MAN WHO CRAWLED

In one of our Gospel Festivals in India, a man paralyzed from his waist down was lying on the ground listening as I spoke of Jesus Christ. He pushed himself up leaning on his arms all the while inching his way around the crowd to get a closer view of the platform. When I spoke in the name of Jesus for the lame to rise up and walk, he tried to get up but fell down. He did it again with the same dismal result. I would never have known these details unless a friend of mine, Pastor Frederick Mwassa from the east coast of Kenya, had been present. He was standing looking at this pitiful sight of a man trying to get up and walk. He told me after the meeting, "Peter, I approached the lame man saying, 'Shall I help you?' The man responded, 'No, I believe the word of Jesus that I have heard preached. I believe it more than I believe in my paralyzed condition. I will walk on my own.'" Again he tried, and this time life flowed to his limbs. He jumped to his feet and came running to the platform while all the people who'd seen him began to weep and cry, and were beside themselves at what they had just witnessed. The Holy Spirit had revealed Jesus to that man. Jesus had given him faith, and no one was going to talk him out of it.

I could relate this story and another person in a similar condition could say and act in exactly the same way, and nothing would happen. It is true that faith responds by acting, that faith without works is dead. But faith doesn't come from imitating the action of someone else; faith comes from Jesus. Don't try to imitate or copy what someone else has done, instead just draw closer to Jesus. Ask the Holy Spirit to reveal Jesus to you more everyday. Jesus' faith, assurance and peace will come into your heart. This is why every miracle testimony is unique, whether a testimony from the Bible or a current one. As each individual connects with Jesus, that person will act out their faith in Him.

Jesus is the key to everything. Our miracle is in Him. *The more we look at our own effort the worse it gets, while the more we look at Jesus the easier it becomes.* I have increasingly made my whole focus to lift up Jesus. The apostle Paul writes, "O foolish Galatians! Who has bewitched you that you should not obey the truth, before whose eyes Jesus Christ was clearly portrayed among you as crucified?" (Galatians 3:1) Faith, miracles, healings and wonders are not produced by methods or faith techniques. These blessings come when people fully see Jesus portrayed. This was Paul's preaching style: to vividly paint a picture of the awesomeness of Jesus.

IT IS A GIFT

Mental believing comes from within our self. We try to achieve a level of soulish concentration where we think we believe something. This is the complete opposite of the faith of God. Look again at this Scripture. "For by grace you have been saved through faith, and that not of yourselves; it is the gift of God, not of works, lest anyone should boast." (Ephesians 2:8-9)

This means:

1. *Faith is "not of ourselves;"*
2. *Faith is "a gift of God;"*
3. *Faith is "not of works;"*
4. *If faith came from ourselves or our works we*

could boast, but since it doesn't, all boasting goes to Jesus.

The next verse sheds light on how real faith comes. "For we are His workmanship, created in Christ Jesus for good works, which God prepared beforehand that we should walk in them." (Ephesians 2:10) Everything we have is because we are new creations in Christ Jesus. We are believers because Jesus Christ, the Author and Finisher of faith, is in us. *We nurture and grow this God-given faith by continually looking unto Jesus.*

Do you work for a "gift?" Obviously not! A gift must be free or it is no longer a gift. Faith is a gift of God.

At times we hear people say, "I have seriously studied and prayed and my faith is growing. I believe I can do great things for God now." This type of speaking is an indication that faith's not at work, because we cannot work for faith and consequently we can't boast in it.

Now, don't misunderstand me. I practice Bible reading, prayer, and spiritual discipline with all my heart. Still we may read and pray diligently and yet not have the faith that moves mountains. Only Jesus can give us this faith. When His peaceful presence touches you, another world will open up to you. It's no longer you trying to have faith. Instead, His faith, the faith of Jesus, is flowing through you. He is our TOTAL MIRACLE SOURCE.

CHAPTER 5

FAITH FLOURISHES BY GRACE

Great faith cannot function under pressure to perform or live up to requirements. As long as the sick or needy person is evaluating: "Am I good enough?" "Have I prayed enough?" "Fasted enough?" "Read the Bible enough?" "Have I shown enough Christian virtues?" faith becomes paralyzed. Often a sick person will question and look for hindrances to their healing. Many try to find something wrong by digging into their past or failures. This short-circuits the operation of faith.

The New Testament draws a stark distinction between grace and law.

Grace is what God has done for us. Law is what we try to do.

Grace is the undeserved, unearned, unmerited favor of God given to us because of Jesus. It is totally focused on God's love providing a free gift to everyone who believes through Jesus Christ. The law focuses on human performance and how good we can do. As long as we look at ourselves and our works we will fall short.

Let's look again at the Roman centurion and the Canaanite woman, the only people to whom Jesus ascribed "great faith." Who were they? They were Gentiles or non-Jewish which means they were not under the Law of Moses. Not only were they not under the Law of Moses, in all likelihood, they were completely ignorant of the law.

FAITH OR LAW

Let me show you how faith cannot operate in combination with the law. The word "faith" is only used twice in the Old Testament; once as a rebuke of the people of Israel (Deuteronomy 32:20), and once in a prophetic promise pertaining to the life of a believer in Jesus (Habakkuk 2:4). The Old Testament was the era of law and rules, which made faith void.

The apostle Paul shows the difference between faith and law. "But before faith came, we were kept under guard by the law, kept for the faith which would afterward be revealed. Therefore the law was our tutor to bring us to Christ, that we might be justified by faith. But after faith has come, we are no longer under a tutor." (Galatians 3:23-25)

I underlined the words "before" and "afterward." These words indicate a specific time. Faith came at a specific time. We know that specific time – it was at the resurrection of Jesus. In order to be saved we must believe that God raised Jesus from the dead (Romans 10:9). Until Jesus rose from the dead such faith was not possible. That's why the New Covenant begins with the resurrection of Jesus. Before that time the law was in effect, but once faith had come the law was no longer necessary.

What is the law? How does it relate to us today? Without giving a lengthy historical analysis, the law is about what we can do. It has to do with self-effort, human performance and living up to a standard that "qualifies" us for God's blessings. The people of Israel tried this and failed miserably.

God's objective with the Law was to show the human inability to live according to God's holy and perfect commandments. Simon Peter said that neither the Pharisees nor their forefathers had been able to comply with God's law no matter how hard they tried to (Acts 15:10). As the law showed us our inability to live up to God's standard, it also prepared us to be willing to receive grace. The more we see our inability, grace becomes our only hope.

Grace is the unmerited, unearned, undeserved favor of God toward people.

"Unmerited" means grace doesn't come by achievements or good things we have done. Being a leader, a pastor or bishop doesn't qualify us for grace. It doesn't come by merit.

"Unearned" indicates that grace is not by our own effort, studies or hard work. Nothing we do can possibly earn us God's blessings.

"Undeserved" simply means that we are unworthy in ourselves of God's favor. If we feel we deserve a blessing, miracle or divine favor we have in a sense disqualified ourselves from that grace.

Faith and law cannot mix. Meanwhile, grace and faith flow together. "For by grace you have been saved through faith, and that not of yourselves; it is the gift of God, not of works, lest anyone should boast." (Ephesians 2:8-9) Do you see how faith is the opposite of human performance?

Let's dissect what we read in Galatians 3:23-25:

1. *The law was "before faith came" (v. 23);*
2. *The law was only until Christ came (v. 24);*
3. *When Jesus came, faith came. Faith is now a Person. Jesus is our faith (v. 23-25);*
4. *Once the Faith (Jesus Christ) has come we no longer obtain anything from God by the law, but through faith (v. 25-26). Everything is available in and through Jesus now.*

THEY DID NOT KNOW THE REQUIREMENTS

This is the key to "great faith." The Roman centurion and the Canaanite woman had never been exposed to the law. They did not know the requirements necessary for a miracle. Real faith cannot function under requirements; it only works when the focus is on Jesus. By focusing on the requirements we will only see our own shortcomings. When we look at Jesus we see His abilities.

Paul asked the Galatians, "Therefore He who supplies the Spirit to you and works miracles among you, does He do it by the works of the law, or by the hearing of faith?" (Galatians 3:5) The answer is obvious. The working of miracles was because of the hearing of faith, the hearing of Jesus Christ.

THE LAW MAKES MIRACLES IMPOSSIBLE

Simply put, those with great faith could have great faith because they didn't know the requirements. They had not read, "...If you diligently obey the voice of the LORD your God, to observe carefully all His commandments which I command you today, that the LORD your God will set you high..." (Deuteronomy 28:1) Once we know that the blessing is dependent on our obedience and careful observing of "all commandments," we know we are disqualified. Who among us has obeyed all of God's Word 24/7?

We read in Joshua 1:8, "This Book of the Law shall not depart from your mouth, but you shall meditate in it day and night, that you may observe to do according to all that is written in it. For then you will make your way prosperous, and then you will have good success." Once we know that prosperity and "good success" are dependent on that we speak, meditate and observe "all that is written," and that we do it "day and night," we quickly must disqualify ourselves from the blessing of God. Is there anyone who has kept a 100% focus on God's Word? Certainly not. That is why Jesus says, "He who is without sin cast the first stone." (John 8:7)

This is the dilemma of the legalistic thinking – no one is qualified. If our miracle depends on us, that we have done enough, prayed enough, worshipped enough, read the Bible enough, and been good enough then we must conclude that the miracle will never happen.

When we look at what we have done, faith is impossible, because faith is about what Jesus has done. The Bible shows us that people who were not under the law received great miracles. Jesus said, "...many widows were in Israel in the days of Elijah, when...there was a great famine throughout all the land; but to none of them was Elijah sent except to Zarephath, in the region of Sidon, to a woman who was a widow. And many lepers were in Israel in the time of Elisha the prophet, and none of them was cleansed except Naaman the Syrian." (Luke 4:25-27)

When Jesus highlighted great miracles from the Old Testament, He focused on two people who were both outside the Law of Moses: a widow without food and a leprous Syrian general. These two were also ignorant of the requirements of the Law.

Faith cannot operate alongside a list of requirements. It only works through Christ. "For the Son of God, Jesus Christ, who was preached among you by us…was not Yes and No, but in Him was Yes. For *all the promises of God in Him are Yes, and in Him Amen*, to the glory of God through us." (2 Corinthians 1:19-20) "All God's promises" means everything God has ever promised. How do we receive these promises? Not by our performance, but in Christ. That way no glory goes to us, but when the miracle manifests it is "to the glory of God through us."

NO MIRACLE FORMULA

This is why new believers receive so easily. They pray for a parking spot and get it. I remember as a young traveling preacher staying in the home of a new believer. When the pastor had asked the congregation if anyone would house the traveling minister during a week-long revival the recently saved businessman and his wife immediately responded, thinking they would have an opportunity to learn more about God. The couple owned a furniture factory and while I was their houseguest, several of the heavy-duty sewing machines used for upholstery broke down. To the amazement of the employees, the owner who just weeks earlier would have sworn and cursed, now laid hands on the sewing machines in Jesus' name, and somehow the sewing machines started working. It boggled my mind. These new believers received so easily.

Why is this situation a rather common scenario?

New believers have not yet been told of the "requirements" for a miracle. Often when new believers pray their only focus is Jesus who can do all things. Then one day we announce a seminar on "How to Receive from God" and we teach "Seven Steps to Victory" or "Ten Secrets to Your Breakthrough." We make the miracle complicated and soon new believers are discouraged. Suddenly the miracle is no longer focused on Jesus – it has become a formula. All too often that formula is all about us and what we must do, how much we must worship, rebuke the devil, study, pray, fast and meditate. Now the new believer realizes he should never have received any answer to prayer at all. After all, he has not lived up to the requirements. Faith is a gift from God but religion makes it a product of what we do. This completely contradicts Paul's teaching that faith does not work in conjunction with human effort.

ARE MIRACLES EASIER OVERSEAS?

People ask me why miracles seem to come so easily overseas. It has nothing to do with "overseas." It has everything to do with whether people have been exposed to legalism or not. Forget the myth that miracles happen overseas. *Miracles happen to people who are not under the curse of legalistic thinking.*

Yes, in our great Gospel Festivals we consistently see the lame walk, the blind see, the deaf hear and we have seen the dead brought back to life. These miracles happen when Jesus is preached to a multitude of non-Christians. These "unbelievers" hear a message that

Jesus is able and willing to help them. I tell the people, "If you don't have faith, or if your faith is small, no problem, we'll ask Jesus to give you faith." You see, we focus only on Jesus and Him crucified. When the people believe this Christ-centered teaching, miracles happen.

Some think we preach about healings and miracles. Really, I do not. I preach about Jesus as our righteousness and what He has already done, and miracles follow. When you preach signs, wonders and miracles you may see some results, but when you preach Jesus our righteousness, signs, wonders and miracles are the inevitable result as faith comes to the people who hear the Gospel.

The same miracles happen to people who have been Christians all their life; if they are willing to come to God without any reliance on their own efforts. The problem is when Christians expect God to heal them because of their own faithfulness or good works. No, we all come to God like little children totally dependent on their parent.

DO YOU QUALIFY?

When people ask me to pray for them, they sometimes say, "Pastor Peter, I have lots of faith." Immediately I am quite sure nothing will happen. You see, people who speak in this manner usually think they have faith based on what they have done. Maybe they prayed a lot, or listened to audio teachings about faith and healing, or read books on the subject. Real faith never looks to our own performance; it only looks to Jesus. The mountain-moving faith has nothing to do with an intellectual knowledge of doctrine. We may know about faith, miracles and healings, but this in itself does not constitute faith.

Maybe you have been inwardly measuring your faith to see if you qualify for a miracle. You will never measure up or qualify. *Look to Jesus, who has already qualified you.* You are not qualified by what you can do, but by what He has done.

One of the most famous miracles recorded in Scripture is the healing of blind Bartimaeus. Jesus said Bartimaeus had faith, "Go your way; your faith has made you well." (Mark 10:52) It's nice to notice that someone has faith, but even more importantly: how did he get it? Someone may suggest that Bartimaeus already had faith before Jesus came, but that does not make sense. If he had faith he would have been healed before Jesus came, because faith always works. We must therefore conclude that before Jesus came on the scene, Bartimaeus did not have faith that his blind eyes would open. It all started when the beggar heard that Jesus was passing by.

Bartimaeus did not recite positive words like, "I'm healed, I'm healed, I'm healed," or "I can see, I can see, I can see." He became *completely Jesus-focused.* Though some tried to discourage him suggesting it was not appropriate for him to boisterously and loudly call for Jesus, he continued all the more crying out, "Jesus, have mercy on me!" (Mark 10:48) Jesus responded to

Bartimaeus, "What do you want Me to do for you?" (Mark 10:51)

Notice, Jesus is not telling Bartimaeus anything that he should do. Instead, Jesus suggests that He will do something. Some today might have told Bartimaeus that he needed to break the spirit of fear, intimidation and blindness over his life. Others may have thought he should go back to the root of the sickness and break that, or some other spiritual exercise that Bartimaeus ought to have done. This is completely foreign to Jesus' healing approach. His question was simply, "What do you want Me to do?" Bartimaeus could obviously not do anything to be healed or he would have already done it. The healing that was about to happen was totally dependent on Jesus.

Jesus never laid a heavy burden or a legalistic thought on a sick and needy person. Instead He helped that hurting person to turn their attention away from their own inability and lack, and onto Jesus who was able to do something about the situation. Maybe you want to lift your hands and praise and give thanks to Jesus right now. Say words like, "Holy Spirit, reveal Jesus more fully to me." As you become COMPLETELY JESUS-FOCUSED His faith begins to flourish in you.

CHAPTER 6

FAITH IS RESTFUL

Faith is easy. It is simply yielding to and resting in Jesus' ability. The apostle Paul asks the Galatian believers, "He who supplies the Spirit to you and works miracles among you, does he do it by the works of the law or by the hearing of faith?" (Galatians 3:5)

Put this question in contemporary language. Do you receive the Holy Spirit and does God work miracles among you by your efforts and struggles? Does it happen by how well you have performed your religious duties? Or do these divine blessings come by hearing of Jesus and His abilities?

As a young new believer, I heard that the next step in my spiritual growth was to receive the baptism of the Holy Spirit. Naturally, I wanted to advance in my newfound life as a believer, and I thought I must have this experience with the Holy Spirit. I was spending three weeks at a Christian youth camp where people told me if I sincerely wanted the baptism of the Holy Spirit I should attend a 7 am prayer meeting. These were beautiful Christian friends and they wanted the best for me. They emphasized that this prayer time was only for those who were sincere in their quest for the Holy Spirit. I was fourteen years old and an early-morning prayer meeting was not really my style, but I wanted to put forth a good effort. Bleary-eyed, I rolled out of bed at five minutes to seven in the morning and rushed to the prayer meeting. We begged and pleaded with the Lord, "Please God, please baptize us in the Holy Spirit." If anyone should have received because of our effort, it should have been us. In fact, one of the young men, Hans, who was the leader of this prayer meeting was an exemplary youth. I felt I was not nearly as "holy" as he. He was the one who woke me up so I would make it in time to the prayer meeting. If anyone should have been rewarded with the baptism of the Holy Spirit, it was Hans. He had a stepbrother who was his complete opposite, named Steve. Steve wasn't saved, and furthermore, was the number one troublemaker at the youth camp. If anything went wrong, any prank, we knew Steve was behind it.

One night this rebellious young man wandered into our evening service. We never knew if he'd show up or not, though the rules of the camp mandated that everybody had to be in attendance. Steve was crying and called out that he needed Jesus. We all thought that was wonderful. We knew he needed salvation considering what a "big sinner" he was. Fifteen minutes after Steve received Jesus as his Savior, he was baptized in the Holy Spirit speaking in other tongues. When we saw this, knowing how thoroughly unsanctified he was, we were a bit unsure. However, we thought, "Well, God is good so maybe this is alright after all." Then, twenty minutes after this experience we heard Steve's voice from the back of the auditorium speaking a message in other tongues prefacing it with "thus saith the Lord."

If you are unfamiliar with this kind of a happening, it is described in Paul's writing to the Corinthians. A message in tongues and interpretation are two out of the nine gifts of the Holy Spirit mentioned there. Steve was giving a message in tongues and interpreting, prophesying to us who felt superior to him spiritually. The word he gave was very powerful and though we sensed it was a word from God we had a tough time receiving it. What business did God have to use such a troublemaker? If anyone should have been prophesying it should have been one of us who had attended the 7 am prayer meeting. We had been begging God and seemingly received nothing. Do you see how a religious legalistic mindset works? The legalistic condemning person hates the undeserved, unearned, unmerited favor of God. "Didn't Steve still need to get sanctified?" you may ask. Of course, but God does not give miracles according to how qualified a person is. He does it by faith. I've seen this scenario repeated hundreds of times. It's the hopeless and the hurting that are touched by Jesus.

All Christian virtues, including humility and sanctification are very important. God's grace will work in us if we allow it to produce these qualities. However, possession of Christian virtues does not earn us points toward a miracle.

As mentioned earlier hundreds of people have approached me saying, "Pastor Peter, pray for me. I have lots of faith. Just ask God to heal me now." I could be wrong, there could be some instance I have forgotten, but I can't think of a single person who approached me proclaiming how much faith they had who actually received their miracle. Faith is not an issue of human performance, but rather of connecting a person with Jesus. *People who are focused on faith rarely receive; those focused on Jesus readily receive.*

ARE YOU GOOD ENOUGH?

That's why the stories of the Canaanite woman and the Roman centurion are so important. Jesus ascribed "great faith" to them. They didn't even know all the requirements for healing. They were Gentiles who had not been exposed to the law of Moses. The less we look at ourselves and the more we look to Jesus, the more faith comes. Faith has nothing to do with our achievement or our worthiness. Questions like "Am I good enough? Do I measure up?" make faith of no effect.

Faith rests in Jesus and His ability. That's why we often see Muslims, Buddhists, and Hindus who know very little about the Bible receive astounding miracles. Though they have never heard of the Book of Genesis, the epistles to the Romans or Galatians, they grasp the simple truth of God's love revealed in Jesus for them. *Once a person connects with Jesus, everything is possible.*

When we forget ourselves and look at Jesus Christ

we become peaceful. Faith is not rules concerning what we must do. When we see Jesus as big as He really is we relax in Him. When Jesus appears great to your inward eyes you automatically start speaking positively, confessing God's Word. In fact, you can't speak negatively when you see Jesus completely as big and awesome. This is entirely opposite of being stressed to live up to expectations, as if God was a scorekeeper in heaven counting points to see if you have shown enough faith to qualify for an answer to your prayers.

Peter Youngren's faith isn't very good; that's why I hook up with Jesus' faith. If it's up to the sick person's faith or the preacher's faith, we don't have much hope. Sometimes people say to me, "Peter, you're such a man of faith." Of course, I like when people say nice things about me, but in myself I'm not a great man of faith. Truthfully, in myself I have little or no faith, but I have experienced thousands of times when Jesus' ability and His faith has flowed through me. Because of Jesus living in me I have full access to His faith. I yield to Him.

It is stressful to pretend faith. If a doctor diagnoses I'm going to die in thirty days, my mind understands the implications of that diagnosis. I can't psych myself into some miracle-working faith; I need the faith of the Son of God. I would want to pray, "Lord, no matter how hard I try to believe, no matter how much I try to put on a good face, I know that Your faith is the only faith that works. Jesus, I just want to draw closer to You. Let Your life, Word, faith and power flow through me."

JESUS IS RELAXED

When Jesus calmed the raging storm, all the disciples were on deck screaming, "We perish! God help us!" All the while Jesus was asleep in the bottom of the boat. We may have foolishly reprimanded Jesus, "Don't You have any sense of responsibility, Jesus? The boat is going under and You're asleep? At least the disciples showed some responsibility and cried for help." If we didn't know any better we would think the disciples were the ones with faith. If the Bible account had said there were thirteen people on the boat and one was asleep, we would have thought the one sleeping was Judas or Thomas or maybe Simon Peter, but not Jesus. The Bible account however is clear that the author and finisher of faith was asleep on a pillow. There's no panic with Jesus.

When Jesus heard that Lazarus was dying we read, "So, when He heard that he was sick, He stayed two more days in the place where He was." (John 11:6) If we didn't know it was Jesus who purposely waited two days we would have thought it was one of the disciples. Possibly it was Judas or Thomas who encouraged this delay. We may have thought that the responsible action of Jesus would have been to hurry to the house of Mary, Martha and Lazarus, and quickly perform the miracle. Again Jesus exemplifies rest. When we lift Him up and we see how great He is and His love fills our hearts we too will be at rest. This restful faith causes tumors to melt and slipped discs, hernias and joints and inflammations to be healed.

Jesus is relaxed in every situation. Consider the feeding of the five thousand. Even though Jesus knew what He was going to do He asked Philip, "What do you think?" Jesus didn't say, "I am the Messiah. I have the revelation. You better start bringing some empty baskets or this miracle is not going to happen." No, Jesus is at rest.

You may have heard a lot of stressful preaching about how you must produce faith. It's one thing for healthy folks to be stressed out, but if you're on your deathbed and get taken into a healing service and once you get there they stress you out with so many instructions, it actually becomes worse than the hospital. That's not Jesus' ministry. For He said, "Come to Me, all you who labor and are heavy laden, and I will give you rest. Take My yoke upon you and learn from Me, for I am gentle and lowly in heart, and *you will find rest for your souls*. For My yoke is easy and My burden is light." (Matthew 11:28-30)

You need not be stressed about the size of your faith. Instead, allow Jesus to get bigger before your inward eyes. Is Jesus big enough to touch your family? To remove your tumor? Big enough for your lung problem, psoriasis, eczema, migraine? Is Jesus big enough to heal your cancer? How big is your Jesus? *Let nothing come between you and Jesus, not even your earnest attempt to have faith*. Be at rest in Jesus!

ALL ABOUT JESUS NOW

Before Jesus' death and resurrection, while we were still in the Old Covenant, Jesus frequently told people, "Your faith has made you whole." Never again are these words spoken once we enter into the New Covenant after Jesus' death and resurrection. Never again are believers told, "Why don't you have faith?" You cannot be a born-again believer and be without faith. Once you are a believer the author and finisher of faith lives inside of you.

These words "your faith has made you whole" were never spoken by the apostles Paul, John or Peter, once Jesus had finished the work of His death and resurrection. Rather, Simon Peter looked at Aeneas who was lame, and said, "Jesus heals you." Philip went to Samaria and "preached Jesus Christ to them." Paul said, "I preach only 'Jesus Christ and Him crucified.'" The whole message and operation of miracles was centered on Jesus. The Holy Spirit glorifies Jesus. When we put the focus on Jesus, what He has done and His ability, the Holy Spirit works with us.

When you receive the healing you need while reading the pages of this book, please don't say, "Peter Youngren's ministry is really powerful." No, we don't want to exalt a ministry; we only want to lift up Jesus. I've heard too many statements like, "I have a ministry for back problems; I have a ministry for deaf ears; I have a ministry for stomach healings." It's about time we say, "I've got Jesus and He is all-sufficient." This way we don't have to seek healing or any specially anointed person, but our pursuit is after the Healer. *If nothing happens at first when we pray then we just draw closer to Jesus and His Word.* We don't blame ourselves or others, but instead we ask the Holy Spirit for an ever clearer revelation of Jesus.

The Book of Hebrews says, "For he who has entered His rest has himself also ceased from his works as God did from His." (Hebrews 4:10) Did you notice that? That rest comes when we cease from our own works. When we stop trying to have faith or earn our miracle we can rest in Jesus' love and power.

CHAPTER 7

FAITH AT THE END OF THE ROAD

Faith flows freely when we are "nothing." When we are "nothing," Jesus is everything. The more "nothing" we are, the more faith will manifest.

Sometimes believers enjoy many repeated victories and blessings. Once we start serving the Lord life gets better. Perhaps we are promoted at work, or our financial position improves; maybe we receive one or several wonderful answers to prayer. As time goes by we are tempted to feel invincible. That is why the Scripture encourages us, "Let him who thinks he stands, take heed lest he fall" (1 Corinthians 10:12). God doesn't want us to "fall," but sometimes it is only when people have experienced their own failure that the words of Jesus, "without Me you can do nothing," become a reality.

One of life's greatest discoveries is that without Jesus we are truly nothing. It is only "with God" that "all things are possible." The contrast is equally true; with man "it is impossible." When we rely on man's power and ability, the situation is hopeless. Good news! When our human hopelessness and nothingness is clear to us, we will find Jesus to be everything we need.

One common denominator between the Canaanite woman and the Roman centurion, those with "great faith," is that they were at the end of themselves.

This is exemplified repeatedly in the Bible. Elijah was filled with fear; he wanted to die because of the threatening words spoken by queen Jezebel. At that low point he met God and walked for forty days in the strength of the divine encounter. Joshua sat with his face between his knees, a posture of discouragement, when he saw the "captain of the Lord's host." This divine encounter changed everything, and Joshua with the people of Israel, marched around the walls of Jericho until they came down flat with the ground. Joseph was in the pit of despair in the dungeon of the prison, at the end of himself, when God exalted him to the palace in Egypt. Simon Peter had utterly failed denying Jesus. In that state of despair, he encountered the Holy Spirit and preached and three thousand were saved. The patriarch Jacob demanded God's blessing, but it was not until he was wounded in his hip and limped, that the blessings came. He had to come to the end of himself.

As long as we think or trust in ourselves as being good enough Christians who live a better life than most, we will end up empty-handed. The truth is we are all miserable failures without Jesus. Seeing our helplessness and hopelessness without Jesus sets the stage for Him to be our source, our everything.

EL SHADDAI

Abraham experienced this truth. God had given him the promise that he would receive a son, but all along Abraham struggled with faith. Each time the Lord would visit him, Abraham would demonstrate his anguish of faith. He tried to convince God that Eleazar, his chief of staff, would be a suitable son of the promise. Later he and Sarah agreed that God's promise would be fulfilled through Abraham having a son with the maid Hagar. God loved and blessed Ishmael, who came through Abraham and Hagar's relationship, but God would not let him be the son of the promise.

Abraham's struggle continued for at least twenty-five years. Why couldn't Isaac have been born when Abraham was seventy-five years old and Sarah sixty-five? Could it be that they had to come to the end of themselves? They had to reach an age where a child was completely beyond all human reason? It had to be impossible? We read; "When Abram was ninety-nine years old, the LORD appeared to Abram and said to him, 'I am Almighty God (El Shaddai); walk before Me and be blameless.'" (Genesis 17:1)

Abraham had tried to be "blameless." The people around him knew he was supposed to receive a son with Sarah, and it looked as if the promise would never be fulfilled. He sure looked like a fool. Abraham tried to make it happen in his own strength, but it only had an opposite effect.

God said, "I am El Shaddai." El means "God," and Shaddai is translated "Almighty." The Hebrew word "shad" means a woman's breast. Some have translated this, "I am the mother-breast-milk God." The picture of God is that of our sustainer or the One who nourishes, in the same way the milk from the mother's breast nourishes the newborn. God was saying, "Abraham, draw from Me all you need. I am your strength, your nourishment, your sustainer, your life giver; cling to Me." The message echoed strong in Abraham's heart, "You have tried in your own strength to be blameless and to make this miracle happen. Now instead just cling to El Shaddai, the Almighty. Rejoice in Him; let God be all that you need."

You will only find genuine faith in a close relationship with the Lord. No real faith exists outside of Jesus Himself. No matter how hard Abraham tried, fought, and struggled for the miracle to happen, he came up with nothing. He was to learn the lesson that each of us must learn; our only hope is in God. Jesus said, "Without Me you can do nothing," but when He is our life, nothing is impossible. Cling to Jesus, just like a baby clings to its mother. Let Jesus be your nourisher and sustainer.

NO MORE DOUBT

Jesus saw a fig tree by the roadside. It had no figs,

which was not surprising because it was not the season for figs. Jesus cursed the fig tree, and the next day when the disciples passed the same way the fig tree was withered. They took note of it with astonishment.

Jesus used this event to teach the disciples to "have God's faith." We read, "So Jesus answered and said to them, 'Have faith in God.'" (Mark 11:22) If you look at the literal translation it is, "Be you having faith of God," or "Have you faith of God." We could simply say, "Have God's faith." Jesus makes it clear to the disciples that to see this kind of wonder it is not enough to have a mental believing; only God's faith will make it happen.

Then He explains how God's faith works, "For assuredly, I say to you, whoever says to this mountain, 'Be removed and be cast into the sea,' and does not doubt in his heart, but believes that those things he says will be done, he will have whatever he says. Therefore I say to you, whatever things you ask when you pray, believe that you receive them, and you will have them." (Mark 11:23-24)

When the faith of God is in operation there is no "doubt" in our hearts. We believe everything we say. This is not humanly possible. If you are hurting in your body, if the doctor has diagnosed you with a serious illness, you can tell your mind, "I believe, I believe." You can ask for prayer, but there is still a little tiny nagging question in your heart, "What if I am not healed?" That's human, and we have all experienced it. Jesus tells us of a faith where there is no doubt in your heart.

Many become disillusioned when they read Jesus' words, "Whatever things you ask when you pray believe that you have received them and you shall have them." (Mark 11:24) They write those words off, saying that it just doesn't work for them. It doesn't work if we try to make it happen through mental believing; it works only through God's faith.

A BAPTIST LADY GOT IT

Long before I ever understood these truths in Scripture, I saw them operating. I was a very young preacher conducting a revival meeting in a little church in eastern Canada. A severely handicapped retired Baptist lady was attending; I think she was intrigued by my message, but she was also very argumentative. She could only move about cautiously while leaning on her walker. After each service she would take me aside and ask questions about healing. I explained to her that it is God's will to heal, and she would argue this point. On another night I would explain to her how Jesus bore every sickness and carried every pain on the cross, which is an awesome truth, but again she would argue this and debate it from a theological position. One night the presence of Jesus swept over the meeting. The Baptist lady had hobbled to the front of the auditorium, her eyes wide open, leaning on her walker. Everyone was caught up in the presence of Jesus, worshiping Him. I forgot to keep my eye on the Baptist lady because I was also caught up with expressing my love toward Jesus. When

I finally opened my eyes I saw this lady at the back of the auditorium, praising and worshiping God with her arms in the air. This went on for some time until she suddenly opened her eyes and a look of astonishment came over her face. I could tell that she was thinking, "Where is my walker?" As it turned out, her walker was still at the front of the auditorium. Now remember that for several years prior she had not moved at all without this support. When the presence of Jesus filled the room she forgot about her walker and moved to the back of the auditorium. She was healed while not even thinking about healing or seeking it, but just overwhelmed in the presence of Jesus. *She came for healing, but instead, she met the Healer.*

Do you see how her doubts vanished in the presence of Jesus? When His love and faith filled her heart, there was no further need for theological arguments. She believed without doubt and the miracle happened.

Ponder again the simple but liberating points I made earlier. These statements may be shocking and turn some of what you have heard previously upside down, yet these statements have brought liberty and freedom and opened the doors wide for Jesus' faith and healing power to flow:

1. *The faith of the sick and needy person is inadequate;*
2. *The faith of the one praying or preaching is inadequate;*
3. *The only adequate faith is Jesus' faith;*

4. *When Jesus' faith becomes our faith, we have mountain-moving faith;*
5. *Our task is to connect people with Jesus.*

You can connect with Jesus. He is ready to touch, lift and bless you. His presence is readily available wherever you are reading these words. Start to worship Him and thank Him right now. He is your El Shaddai. Call on Him; He will answer you.

The expression in Hebrews 12:2 is beautiful, "Looking unto Jesus, the author and finisher of faith." We don't look to Jesus, which would indicate that He is at some distance. Rather we are told to look unto Jesus. This indicates He is right here. We are like a baby looking unto its mother, drawing strength from the mother's breast. Jesus is our life, and when we pray it is His life we receive. This is greater than a miracle; it is Jesus Himself, who is the source of every miracle, living in us.

PRAYER

"God, I come to You only trusting in what Jesus has done for me. Jesus, I believe You put my sins away by Your death on the cross. I believe You were wounded for my sins and that You bore my sickness and disease in Your body on the cross. Jesus, by Your stripes I have been healed. Thank You that You are the source of all I need. Holy Spirit, reveal Jesus more fully to me. Let Jesus become so great that any circumstance, situation or sickness will pale in comparison.

Thank You, Jesus, for Your miracle life and power flowing through me. I promise to give all the praise only to You for all that You have done. Thank You, Jesus. Amen."

CELEBRATE
Jesus International

CELEBRATING LIFE WITH JESUS

ABOUT THE AUTHOR

Passion for the unreached has taken Peter Youngren to more than 80 nations. He has led evangelistic Gospel Festivals with crowds of up to 600,000 attending a single service. In addition, over 246,000 pastors and leaders have attended his training seminars. Hundreds of missionaries are supported around the world on an ongoing basis. As founder of "Celebrate Jesus International," "Celebrate Magazine," "Celebrating Life with Jesus" TV program seen around the world, "Celebration Bible College" and the "Celebration Churches," Peter Youngren is committed to the Gospel reaching the entire earth before the return of Jesus Christ.

Millions are reached via TV, literature and Gospel Festivals

Gospel Festival in the Horn of Africa

CELEBRATING LIFE WITH JESUS

CELEBRATE
Jesus International

AUDIO CD FAVORITES

Sit, Walk, Stand (4cd) Three simple words take on a whole new perspective. An all-time classic!
$US 24.00

The Exalted Jesus (3cd) You have known the babe in the manger, the crucified Savior and the risen Lord. What about the exalted Jesus? Discover who Jesus is to you today.
$US 18.00

The Gospel in Action (5cd) 5 nights of miracles in Guyana. "I have never heard such authority in preaching" is a common remark about this series.
$US 30.00

The Therapeutic Effects of the Cross (4cd) There is so much more to the cross than you ever imagined. Experience the therapy that only comes through the cross of Jesus!
$US 24.00

When Life is Tough (4cd) Discover how the reality of Christ in you can turn tombstones into stepping stones!
$US 24.00

How Grace Works Amazingly in You (6cd) Only God's grace produces holiness, maturity and miracles.
$US 36.00

The Real Bible Code(2cd) Peter Youngren unveils principles that will make every Bible study a treasure hunt.
$US 14.00

Easy Access to Jesus (3cd) This message is crucial because God's heart is that His blessings would be easily accessed by everyone.
$US 18.00

To order any of these items or for a complete listing of our merchandise please visit www.peteryoungren.org or call 1.905.646.0970 / 1.888.628.8241 (toll-free in North America)

CELEBRATE
Jesus International

CELEBRATING LIFE WITH JESUS

VISIT US TODAY!

For more information on any aspect of the Celebration ministry of Dr. Peter Youngren, visit our website today at www.PeterYoungren.org or call 1.905.646.0970 / 1-888-628-8241 toll-free in North America. We are here for you!

- Watch our worldwide television broadcast online!
- Order your favorite merchandise online!
- Check out our most recent Gospel activities online!
- Read Pastor Peter's recent thoughts on his online blog and join a global community commenting and sharing your thoughts with believers from all over the world!
- Find out where Peter will be next in his online schedule!
- Sign up to receive Celebrate e-Newsletters!
- Donate to the work the Lord is doing around the world!

Most of all we appreciate you and the love and support you have shown. Thank you! You mean more to us than you will ever know.